PLEASING

GOD

IN OUR

WORSHIP

TODAY'S
ISSUES

PLEASING

GOD

IN OUR

WORSHIP

R O B E R T
G O D F R E Y

CROSSWAY BOOKS • WHEATON, ILLINOIS
A DIVISION OF GOOD NEWS PUBLISHERS

Pleasing God in Our Worship

Copyright © 1999 by the Alliance of Confessing
Evangelicals

Published by Crossway Books
a division of Good News Publishers
1300 Crescent Street
Wheaton, Illinois 60187

First printing, 1999

Printed in the United States of America

The Alliance of Confessing Evangelicals exists to call the
church, amidst our dying culture, to repent of its worldli-
ness, to recover and confess the truth of God's Word as
did the Reformers, and to see that truth embodied in doc-
trine, worship and life.

Library of Congress Cataloging-in-Publication Data
Godfrey, Robert, 1945-
    Pleasing God in our worship / Robert Godfrey.
    p.   cm. — (Today's issues)
    Includes bibliographical references.
    ISBN 1-58134-079-6
    1. Worship—Biblical teaching.   I. Title.
BS680.W78G63   1999
264—dc21
                                 99-12506
                                       CIP

13	12	11	10	09	08	07	06	05	04	03	02	01	00
15	14	13	12	11	10	9	8	7	6	5	4	3	

CONTENTS

PREFACE

These are not good days for the evangelical church, and anyone who steps back from what is going on for a moment to try to evaluate our life and times will understand that.

In the last few years a number of important books have been published all trying to understand what is happening, and they are saying much the same thing even though the authors come from fairly different backgrounds and are doing different work. One is by David F. Wells, a theology professor at Gordon-Conwell Theological Seminary in Massachusetts. It is called *No Place for Truth*. A second is by Michael Scott Horton, vice president of the Alliance of Confessing Evangelicals. His book is called *Power Religion*. The third is by the well-known pastor of Grace Community Church in California, John F. MacArthur. It is called *Ashamed of the Gospel*. Each of these authors is writing about the evangelical church, not the liberal church, and a person can get an idea of what each is saying from the titles alone.

Yet the subtitles are even more revealing. The subtitle of Wells's book reads *Or Whatever Happened to Evangelical Theology?* The subtitle of Horton's book is *The Selling Out of the Evangelical Church*. The subtitle of John MacArthur's work proclaims, *When the Church Becomes Like the World*.

When you put these together, you realize that these careful observers of the current church scene perceive that today evangelicalism is seriously off base because it has abandoned its evangelical truth-heritage. The thesis of David Wells's book is that the evangelical church is either dead or dying as a significant religious force because it has forgotten what it stands for. Instead of trying to do God's work in God's way, it is trying to build a prosperous earthly kingdom with secular tools. Thus, in spite of our apparent success we have been "living in a fool's paradise," Wells declared in an address to the National Association of Evangelicals in 1995.

John H. Armstrong, a founding member of the Alliance of Confessing Evangelicals, has edited a volume titled *The Coming Evangelical Crisis*. When he was asked not long afterwards whether he thought the crisis was still coming or is actually here, he admitted that in his judgment the crisis is already upon us.

The Alliance of Confessing Evangelicals is addressing this problem through seminars and conferences, radio programs, *modern* REFORMATION magazine, Reformation Societies, and scholarly writings. The series of booklets on today's issues is a further effort along these same lines. If you are troubled by the state of today's church and are helped by these booklets, we invite you to contact the Alliance at 1716 Spruce Street, Philadelphia, PA 19103. You can also phone us at 215-546-3696 or visit the Alliance at our website: www.AllianceNet. org. We would like to work with you under God "for a modern Reformation."

James Montgomery Boice
President, Alliance of Confessing Evangelicals
Series Editor

ONE

———

Worship
Wars

You may have heard the story of two men debating issues of worship. They had quite different ideas on the subject and were unable to persuade one another. At the end of the frustrating discussion one of the men said to the other, "Well, you worship God in your way, and I will worship him in his."

We may smile at that comment, but we need to remember how varied are the forms of worship that churches have practiced and how vehement debate over worship sometimes has been. The debate over the use of icons in the eighth and ninth centuries led to violence in the Eastern church. Differences over worship in the sixteenth century were part of what divided Protestant from Roman Catholic Christianity, a division that continues to our day.

Among contemporary Protestants we find significant differences in worship. Some forms of worship are filled with formal ceremony and ritual, while others are very casual and informal. Some are noisy and boisterous, while others are quiet and contemplative. Some take place in beautiful cathedrals, while others occur in warehouses or fields. In the midst of such diversity Christians sometimes ask if worship is simply a matter of taste. Are all forms of worship equally pleasing to God as long as the worshipers are sincere? Or are some ways of worship acceptable and others not?

The question of what pleases God in worship comes with special urgency in our time since in the last few decades American Protestants have seen more changes in worship forms than in any similar period since the sixteenth century. The result is that some congregations and denominations have experienced serious conflicts over worship. Churches have split and individuals have moved from congregation to congregation, all over different views of worship.

Some of the differences over worship seem rather superficial though they may generate heated debates.

• Should we use a songbook or an overhead projector?

• Should we sit on pews or folding chairs?

More serious differences have led to what some have called the "worship wars" of our time.

• What style of music should we use?

• What kind of instruments should we play?

• How should we pray?

• What kind of preaching is appropriate?

Often these differences rest on the question of whether services should be oriented to the unchurched visitor or the faithful church member.

Differences over worship can also reflect quite different theologies and methodologies in the Christian community. For that reason the Alliance of Confessing Evangelicals briefly addressed the issue of worship in its Cambridge Declaration. The Declaration stated as its basic concern: "Evangelical churches today are increasingly dominated by the spirit of this age rather than by the Spirit of Christ. As evangelicals, we call ourselves to repent of this sin and to recover the historic Christian faith."

The Declaration then expanded on this concern in relation to the great themes of the Protestant

Reformation: Scripture alone, Christ alone, grace alone, faith alone, and glory to God alone. Under that last theme, glory to God alone, the Declaration spoke of worship:

> The loss of God's centrality in the life of today's church is common and lamentable. It is this loss that allows us to transform worship into entertainment, gospel preaching into marketing, believing into technique, being good into feeling good about ourselves, and faithfulness into being successful. . . . We must focus on God in our worship, rather than the satisfaction of our personal needs. God is sovereign in worship; we are not. Our concern must be for God's kingdom, not our own empires, popularity or success.

The Declaration's proper concern for right worship should be the concern of every Christian. We need to think carefully about worship and then ensure that our worship is pleasing to God. We need scriptural principles to show us the way.

This study is intended to help Christians begin to think about worship from a biblical point of view. It will not answer every question about worship, but it will seek to build a foundation for understanding and evaluating worship. In the process of thinking biblically about worship, our own worship will become a more meaningful experience.

TWO

The Need for
True Worship

All Christians need to cultivate a life with God that
is growing and developing. If we are not growing,
we will stagnate or die. The corporate, official worship of God's people is a crucial and essential means
God has given to help us grow. Think of the words
of Hebrews 10:19-22:

> *Therefore, brothers, since we have confidence
> to enter the Most Holy Place by the blood of
> Jesus, by a new and living way opened for us
> through the curtain, that is, his body, and
> since we have a great high priest over the
> house of God, let us draw near to God with a
> sincere heart in full assurance of faith, having
> our hearts sprinkled to cleanse us from a
> guilty conscience and having our bodies
> washed with pure water.*

This passage calls Christians to draw near to God
through Christ since, even as Christians, we experience a distance between ourselves and God that
only the work of Christ can bridge. We need to
draw near to him personally and individually in
devotion, meditation, and prayer; but we also
need to draw near to him by meeting with him in
the fellowship of his people, where God promises
to be especially present (Matt. 18:20). We meet

with God when the people of God meet together, pray together, sing together, and listen to his Word together.

Christianity is a religion in which individuals become an integral part of Christ's body. We are not just an association of individuals, but we are organically connected to one another (1 Cor. 12:12-27; Eph. 1:22-23). We express that we are the body of Christ, especially when we meet God together in public worship.

Worshiping False Gods

John Calvin rightly called the human heart "a factory of idolatry," meaning that faithful worship does not come naturally to fallen human beings. Sinners become idolaters because God has so deeply planted the need for himself in human beings that when we do not know the true God, we invent false gods, false religion, and false worship. God warns against such idolatrous worship in the first commandment: "You shall have no other gods before me." The idolatrous worship of false gods is condemned throughout the Bible.

Worshiping the True God Falsely

We need to listen to the call of Scripture to promote holy worship and flee idolatry. But the worship of false gods is not the only kind of idolatry condemned in the Bible. The second commandment teaches us that idolatry is not only a matter of worshiping false gods, which is prohibited in the first commandment. It is also a matter of worshiping the true God falsely. The second commandment says, "You shall not make for yourself an idol in the form of anything in heaven above or on the earth beneath or in the waters below. You shall not bow down to them or worship them; for I, the LORD your God, am a jealous God, punishing the children for the sins of the fathers to the third and fourth generation of those who hate me, but showing love to thousands of those who love me and keep my commandments" (Exod. 20:4-6).

This commandment clearly forbids the use of images of God in worship, but it also implicitly forbids all human invention in worship. The prohibition against images means that we must worship the true God only in ways that please him. The people of Israel claimed they were worshiping the Lord as the true God when they fashioned the golden calf. They regarded the image as Jehovah (Exod. 32:5-6). But such false worship offended God and brought judgment on the people.

The story of the golden calf reminds us that God's own people can fall into idolatry in their worship of him. We may want to be creative and inventive in worship, but that creativity can lead to idolatry. Repeatedly in the Old Testament God judged his people for false worship. Aaron's sons Nadab and Abihu were struck dead for offering "unauthorized fire before the LORD, contrary to his command" (Lev. 10:1). Jeroboam, the first king of the northern kingdom of Israel, and his heirs were consistently criticized as idolaters because of images and false temples and services dedicated to the Lord. The people of God were rebuked in these instances not for worshiping false gods, but for worshiping the true God falsely.

The New Testament also warns against pleasing ourselves with false worship. Paul wrote to the Colossians condemning their novelties and experiments with "self-imposed worship" (Col. 2:23). Jesus warned against allowing traditions to dominate and subvert the Word of God: "Thus you nullify the word of God for the sake of your tradition" (Matt. 15:6). Jesus was not speaking about worship when he made that statement, but then he used Isaiah 29:13, which is about worship, to support his words:

> *These people honor me with their lips,*
> *but their hearts are far from me.*
> *They worship me in vain;*
> *their teachings are but rules*
> *taught by men. (vv. 8-9)*

He was saying that our service to God, whether in life generally or in corporate worship, must not be determined by tradition but must follow the teaching of God in the Bible.

Paul specifically warned the Corinthians against false worship in the way they were administering the Lord's Supper. The sins and errors that infected their worship led Paul to charge them with destroying that sacrament: "When you come together, it is not the Lord's Supper you eat . . ." (1 Cor. 11:20). In fact, God cares so much about worship that Paul records that God visited judgment on the Corinthians for their abuses in worship related to that sacrament: "That is why many among you are weak and sick, and a number of you have fallen asleep" (v. 30).

The Bible reminds us that neither our instincts nor our traditions nor our experiments are reliable guides to worship. The Bible itself is our only reliable guide. One of the ironies of our time is that many Christians who affirm the inerrancy of the Bible do not really study it to find out what it says about worship. We must search the Scriptures to find God's will to guide us in our worship. The Cambridge Declaration made this point: "The Bible alone teaches all that is necessary for our salvation from sin and is the standard by which all Christian behavior must be measured."

THREE

The Character
of Worship

To learn how to worship God in a way that will please God rather than offend him and be judged by him, we must begin by understanding the Bible's definition of what worship is. The Bible uses the word *worship* in at least three important ways.

Personal and Corporate Worship

First, worship can refer to the whole life of the Christian. We are to live our lives *for* God and *under* God. We should seek to have all we do become loving service to him. Paul had this sense of worship in mind when he wrote at the beginning of the application section of the book of Romans, "Therefore, I urge you, brothers, in view of God's mercy, to offer your bodies as living sacrifices, holy and pleasing to God—which is your spiritual worship. Do not conform any longer to the pattern of this world, but be transformed by the renewing of your mind" (12:1-2). In these verses all life is looked upon as worship.

Second, worship can refer to those personal times of prayer, praise, reflection, or Bible reading when we focus on God. David worshiped as he prayed and sang alone at night:

On my bed I remember you;
I think of you through the
watches of the night.
Because you are my help,
I sing in the shadow of
your wings. (Ps. 63:6-7)

Third, worship can refer to times when Christians gather officially as a congregation to praise God. This form of worship is commended and commanded in the Scriptures. "Let us not give up meeting together, as some are in the habit of doing, but let us encourage one another—and all the more as you see the Day approaching" (Heb. 10:25). The Psalms celebrate this privilege of corporate worship:

Praise the LORD.
I will extol the LORD
with all my heart
in the council of the upright
and in the assembly. (Ps. 111:1)

Clearly God wants his people to gather as congregations, expressing that they are the body of Christ as they worship him with one another.

This third use of worship, corporate worship, deserves special attention for two reasons. First, the arena of corporate worship is where most of the worship wars are being fought. Changes in corporate worship need careful examination in our time.

Second, many Christians seem to have a measure of prejudice against corporate worship as a priority in the lives of believers. They seem to believe that the official worship of the church is not very important. They find it too formal and impersonal. They feel that individual times of prayer and Bible reading or small group experiences are much more important in cultivating nearness to God than is corporate worship. Some of the recent changes in corporate worship reflect an effort to make it more like a small group activity. However, as we examine the Bible's teaching about worship and its content, we will see that corporate worship is vitally important for every obedient and growing Christian.

A Critical Text: Hebrews 12:28-29

The book of Hebrews is particularly important here because it shows the connection between the worship of the Old Testament and the worship of the New Testament, and also because it draws attention to the uniqueness of our worship as the New Testament people of God. Hebrews 12:28-29 states:

> Therefore, since we are receiving a kingdom that cannot be shaken, let us be thankful, and so worship God acceptably with reverence and awe, for our God is a consuming fire.

This passage directs us to two key elements for our thinking about worship: first, the character of God as the object of our worship, and second, our response to God in worship.

1. *The Character of God.* The first truth about God's nature that we need always to remember in worship is that *our God is a Trinity.* The one God exists eternally in three persons—Father, Son, and Holy Spirit. This aspect of God's nature is not explicit in Hebrews 12:28-29, but it is pointed to in the immediate context. Thus Hebrews 12:23-24 reminds us that in worship we come by faith to the living God and to Jesus who is "the mediator of a new covenant." Here two of the persons of the Trinity are distinguished.

As our God is triune, so our worship must be trinitarian. God in his unity is a proper object of worship, but so too are each of the persons of the Godhead. We worship God, and we also worship the Father, the Son, and the Holy Spirit. In worshiping any of the divine persons we worship the whole Godhead, for God is one.

Our worship may focus on any one of the divine persons at particular points because the Bible itself shows us that each person of the Trinity is associated with certain divine acts particularly. For example, in the Bible the Father is particularly linked to the planning of salvation in order to reconcile sinners to himself. The Son is linked to accomplishing salvation as the God-man living, dying, and rising in the place of sinners. The Spirit is linked to applying salvation, drawing sinners to Christ, and giving them faith and new life.

Christian worship reflects the Bible's emphasis on the work of each person in the Godhead. The Father is particularly the object of our worship. We usually pray, as Jesus taught us, "Our Father." The Son is the mediator of our worship. Jesus opened the way to the Father for us by his saving work, and we always come to the Father in his name. The Spirit empowers and blesses our worship. He warms our hearts and draws us, not to himself, but to Jesus and his Word. The very nature of God leads us to worship the Father through the Son by the Holy Spirit.

The second aspect of God's character that we see explicitly in Hebrews 12:28-29 is that *God is a saving God*. He has prepared an unshakable kingdom of eternal life for those who belong to him. This kingdom belongs to Jesus Christ (Heb. 1:8), who is the Savior of his people and the mediator between man and God in all our worship. Jesus and his Gospel must always stand at the heart of our worship. We must remember that he is the eternal second person of the Trinity, made man to be our Savior. We must rejoice in his perfect life of obedience for us, in his death on the cross where he bore all our sins, and in his glorious resurrection to be our ever-living Savior and High Priest. Worship fails utterly if Jesus Christ is not at the center. His person and work must light up the worship of his people. He makes God fully known and fully accessible to us. He is our refuge and strength, a very present help in times of trouble (Ps. 46:1). He saves us from our sins, and our worship must celebrate him.

The third aspect of God's character that we see in Hebrews 12 is that *God is a holy God*, one who is jealous for his worship. He is a God who stands in judgment of sin and calls for holy living among his people. Hebrews is quoting Deuteronomy 4 when it states that God is "a consuming fire." Deuteronomy 4 calls the people of God to faithfulness in all of their lives, but especially in worship: "Be careful not to forget the covenant of the LORD your God that he made with you; do not make for yourselves an idol in the form of anything the LORD your God has forbidden. For the Lord your God is a consuming fire, a jealous God" (vv. 23-24).

This passage in Deuteronomy clearly rests on the second of the Ten Commandments, which forbids false worship, as we have seen. The holy character of God must echo as clearly through our worship as does the saving character of God.

These passages show that the Lord takes his worship very seriously. They show us very specifically that our worship must reflect both God's great saving work in Christ and his holy zeal for the purity of worship. Only such worship will be acceptable to him. When Hebrews 12:28 speaks of acceptable worship, it means worship that is first and foremost acceptable to God.

This priority needs to be reaffirmed especially today. Too often today when people speak of acceptable worship they mean worship that is acceptable to themselves or perhaps acceptable especially to the unchurched. While worship must communicate clearly to the gathered congregation, the Bible insists that worship must above all be acceptable to God. And we must always remember that we can only know what is acceptable to God by a careful study of his Word.

2. *Our Response to God.* How should we respond in worship to this holy, saving God? Hebrews 12 not only specifies the character of God for us in worship, but it also clarifies the character of our response to God: our worship is to be characterized by thankfulness and awe. Especially in reaction to God's saving work, we are to be thankful and filled with joy. The Psalms often express this response:

> *Sing for joy to God our strength;*
> *Shout aloud to the God of*
> *Jacob! (Ps. 81:1)*

> *Come, let us sing for joy to the* LORD;
> *let us shout aloud to the*
> *Rock of our salvation.*
> *Let us come before him*
> *with thanksgiving*
> *and extol him with music*
> *and song. (Ps. 95:1-2)*

> *Serve the* LORD *with gladness;*
> *come before him with*
> *joyful songs. (Ps. 100:2)*

> *For you make me glad*
> *by your deeds, O* LORD;
> *I sing for joy at the works*
> *of your hands. (Ps. 92:4)*

Our response to God ought to be one of great joy and gladness for the saving work of Jesus. Thankfulness should manifest itself in many parts of the worship service. The Psalms remind us that music is one of the key ways in which we express our joy and thankfulness to God. (We will look more fully at music in worship later in our study.) Other manifestations of thankfulness include prayer and heartfelt response to the preached Word.

In response particularly to the holiness of God we experience awe and reverence before him. The Psalms also show us this reaction:

> Worship the LORD
> in the splendor of his holiness;
> tremble before him,
> all the earth. (Ps. 96:9)

> The LORD reigns,
> let the nations tremble;
> he sits enthroned between
>   the cherubim, let the
>   earth shake.
> Great is the LORD in Zion;
> he is exalted over all the nations.
> Let them praise your great and
>   awesome name—he is holy.
> The King is mighty, he loves
>   justice—you have established
>   equity;
> in Jacob you have done what
> is just and right.
> Exalt the LORD our God
> and worship at his footstool;
> he is holy. (Ps. 99:1-5)

At times in worship there must be serious, sober reflection. As we meet with the God who created heaven and earth, who gave the Law at Mount Sinai, and who visited his wrath against sin on his Son at Calvary, we must be filled with reverent awe. We should quite literally be awestruck when we come into God's presence in worship. Real reverence is never stodgy or dull but is profound and moving.

Today these two responses, joy and reverence, are frequently set in opposition to one another. One kind of worship is called joyful, uplifting, and exuberant, while another kind is called reverent, sedate, respectful. However, in the Scriptures joy and reverence are not antithetical but always complementary. Worship can be joyfully reverent and reverently joyful. Joy and reverence should always be united in our worship.

> *Serve the LORD with fear*
> *and rejoice with trembling.* (Ps. 2:11)

> *The LORD reigns, let the earth be glad;*
> *let the distant shores rejoice.*
> *Clouds and thick darkness*
> *surround him;*
> *righteousness and justice are*
> *the foundation of his throne.*
> *Fire goes before him*
> *and consumes his foes on every side.*
> *His lightning lights up the world;*
> *the earth sees and trembles. . . .*
> *Zion hears and rejoices*
> *and the villages of Judah are glad*
> *because of your judgments,*
> *O LORD.* (Ps. 97:1-4, 8)

> *He provided redemption for his people;*
> *he ordained his covenant forever—*
> *holy and awesome is his name.* (Ps. 111:9)

This combination of joy and awe may not always be easy to achieve, but it must be our goal. We must remember that reverence does not always mean quiet, and joy does not always mean noise. Joy and reverence are first of all attitudes of the heart for which we seek appropriate expressions in worship. Joy may be intense in the singing of a very quiet song. Reverence may be expressed in loud singing.

Traditional Protestant worship has probably been strong on reverence, and what has been called "contemporary worship" often seems enthusiastically joyful. But proponents of each approach must ask whether their views achieve a biblical balance. Traditional worship may proceed so mechanically and formalistically that emotion seems absent. Contemporary worship may be so insistent on fun and excitement that reverence and joy seem lost.

As we seek balance we must begin by remembering that corporate worship is meeting with our God, who is a consuming fire; and for that to happen, we must know God's will for how we are to worship. That knowledge comes only through knowing his Word.

FOUR

Worship and the Word

The churches of the Reformation (and to a significant extent also the churches before the Reformation) not only sought to have the Bible guide their worship, but also sought to fill worship with the Word of God. This is because the Word not only instructs us but is also the means through which we draw near to God. We know, serve, and worship God through his Word. It is also "a lamp to my feet and a light for my path" (Ps. 119:105) in worship.

How is the Word to be present and fill our worship? As the Bible shows, the Word is present in several forms.

Reading God's Word

The most obvious is the reading of the Word. This Word should be a distinct and central part of worship. Paul wrote to Timothy, "devote yourself to the public reading of Scripture, to preaching and to teaching" (1 Tim. 4:13). Here the reading of the Bible is given an importance that is coordinate to preaching and teaching. Too many churches today seem content with reading at most only a few verses of the Bible. In times past, significant sections of several parts of the Bible were read in worship services. In Puritan times several chapters were usually read in each service.

The Bible makes no rule on how much Scripture must be read in any one worship service, but do we really love the Word of God if we are content consistently to hear only a verse or two?

Praying God's Word

The Word should also fill our prayers. The greatest prayers of the church are rich in the language of the Bible itself, offering God's Word back to him in prayer. The words of the Bible should inform our prayers with the truth of God, the promises of God, and the blessings of God on his people. Today much of what passes for prayer in our churches is mere repetitive and shallow talk because of wanting to sound informal and casual. And often prayer becomes only a list of requests to God. Even worse, in some churches prayer has all but disappeared because many say that pastoral prayers are too boring to have in the service.

Surely we should treasure the privilege of speaking to God together as his people and should do so in a manner that shows that his Word has filled our minds and hearts.

Singing God's Word

The Word should be the basis of our singing. At the very least the songs of the church should recount the truths of God's saving work. Primary attention should be given to the content of songs, measuring lyrics by what is scriptural. Often in the history of the church the Psalms of the Old Testament have formed either all or at least a significant part of the praise of God's people. Surely our worship is impoverished today by the relative absence of the Psalms from most worship services in most churches. Singing the Psalms is a wonderful way of hiding the Word of God in our hearts and is a certain way of pleasing the Lord who inspired them and gave them to his people for their good. (We will look at the content of our singing in greater detail later.)

The Word and the Sacraments

The Word must be present in the sacraments of the church—baptism and the Lord's Supper. Augustine called the sacraments "the visible word," which is a helpful way of thinking about them. They are not strange ceremonies that distract from Christ and the Word, but they are precisely another way in which God communicates his Word. The water of baptism speaks of our need for the blood of Christ to cleanse us (Tit. 3:5). The bread and wine of the Lord's Supper speak of our need for the body and blood of Christ to nourish us to eternal life (John 6:53-56). The sacraments bring the very core of the Word, the Gospel of Jesus, into the service.

The Preaching of the Word

Finally, the Word must be present in the preaching of the church. Preaching is the verbal communication of God's Word, applying it to the lives of God's people. The preacher is a minister of the Word of God. His responsibility is to study the Word and then to teach and apply the Word as a central act of worship. God comes to his people and speaks to his people in the faithful preaching of his Word. As the Second Helvetic Confession says, "The preaching of the Word of God is the Word of God." When we hear a faithful sermon, we are hearing Christ speak to us and call us to faith and repentance.

Romans 10:14 actually says, "How, then, can they call on the one they have not believed in? And how can they believe in the one whom they have not heard? And how can they hear without someone preaching to them?" Paul is saying that faith comes by hearing the very words of Jesus in the faithful words of the preacher.

Historically the church has often called preaching (along with the sacraments) a "means of grace." A means of grace is an institution of the Lord by which he has promised to bless his faithful people and help them grow in grace. Preaching, then, is not an opportunity for a preacher to offer opinions or to be amusing, but it is the institution God has appointed and uses for communicating his Word. Where that Word is heard and believed, the blessing of the Lord will always be present. The people of God will grow in knowing the forgiving mercy of God and in knowing God's will for them. Worship ordered according to God's Word features preaching as the most vital element of corporate worship, essential for the life of the people of God.

One of the tragedies of our time is that many pulpits are filled with stories or popular psychology instead of the Bible and its truth. Sometimes preaching is supplemented or even replaced by drama or dance as if they could substitute for preaching. Drama and dance were well-known media for communication in the ancient world, but the apostles and the New Testament church did not use them. Rather, the church used speaking—what Paul calls the "foolishness of what was preached" (1 Cor. 1:21-23)—to communicate Christ. The New Testament gives no hint that drama or dance would be appropriate to Christian worship.

We often hear today that we live in a visual culture where speaking has lost its power and relevance. We need drama or dance or videos to connect with people in our time, some argue. But Paul's world was also visually oriented. Pagan temples had impressive images and rituals. Theater and drama were much more important then than now. Yet the church used preaching to communicate the Gospel, convinced that preaching communicated Christ who was himself "the power of God and the wisdom of God" (1 Cor. 1:24). The church has always been a church of the Book, the verbal revelation of God.

The church also needs preachers who will open up the Scriptures, because Christians always need to hear what God is saying in his Word and how that Word draws them nearer to him. The world offers an abundance of entertaining stories and helpful hints on feeling good. But the church needs the voice of God. As the Cambridge Declaration says, "The Bible, therefore, must be taught and preached in the church. Sermons must be expositions of the Bible and its teachings, not expressions of the preacher's opinions or the ideas of the age."

Faithful preaching not only opens up the Word of God. It also finds God's Law and Gospel in the Word. Week by week Christians need to hear the demand of God to live holy lives. They need the Word of God preached in order to be challenged to grow in love and obedience. Such preaching will not enhance our self-esteem before God, but it will convict us of our sin and our need for a Savior. The ministry of the Law is in the first place a ministry of death, convincing us of our helplessness and driving us to Christ as our only refuge. And week by week Christians need to hear of the cross of Jesus Christ where he bore their sins. We must have the Gospel repeated for us so that we see the complete provision of salvation for us in the death and resurrection of Jesus Christ. We need to be crushed by the Law and called to faith in the Gospel. Word-centered preaching brings us to God.

If we really delight in the Word and seek worship that is filled with the Word, many of the tensions and problems that surround worship today will begin to sort themselves out. We cannot claim to love the Word and be content with its absence from worship. We will want to hear it in reading and preaching, see it in the sacraments, and sing it in our songs.

If we are not interested in the Word of God, can we really be interested in God?

FIVE

Leadership in Worship

Discussion of the Word in worship leads naturally to the subject of leadership in worship. The classic pattern of Protestant worship was for the minister to lead the worship. That pattern arose from the teaching of the New Testament, since out of the congregation God called pastors and teachers to be set apart for leadership roles. "It was he [Christ] who gave some to be apostles, some to be prophets, some to be evangelists, and some to be pastors and teachers, to prepare God's people for works of service" (Eph. 4:11-12).

Called to Ministry

Paul elaborated upon that call to ministry in his personal advice to Timothy: "All Scripture is God-breathed and is useful for teaching, rebuking, correcting and training in righteousness, so that the man of God may be thoroughly equipped for every good work. . . . Preach the Word; be prepared in season and out of season; correct, rebuke and encourage—with great patience and careful instruction . . . keep your head in all situations, endure hardship, do the work of an evangelist, discharge all the duties of your ministry" (2 Tim. 3:16; 4:2, 5). Here is Paul's charge to a minister to be faithful in his teaching and leadership in the Christian community, a charge that related to worship as well as to the whole of Timothy's service to the Lord.

In light of the responsibilities of the office of pastor and teacher, churches must not only call faithful men, but must also when possible provide special education for them. Most universities and, later, seminaries were started to educate church leaders. The foundation of such education rested on the conviction that a thorough knowledge of the Bible and theology was a vital need for preachers. Today when the education of congregations and the population generally is much higher than in earlier generations, the need for well-educated ministers of the Word is stronger than ever.

Two Objections

Today at least two objections are raised against the exercise of leadership by carefully educated and called leaders in worship. The first reflects an anti-intellectual tendency in some Christian circles. It suggests that education kills a man's zeal. It argues that the Holy Spirit will help a man understand the Bible but a school will only undermine his passion. This notion is unbiblical since the Bible repeatedly calls for the people of God to *know* God and his will. Hosea wrote in the name of God, "my people are destroyed from lack of knowledge" (Hos. 4:6). Isaiah recorded the complaint of God that "The ox knows his master, the donkey his owner's manger, but Israel does not know, my people do not understand" (Isa. 1:3). He looked forward to a day when many will say:

> "Come, let us go up to the mountain of the LORD, to the house of the God of Jacob. He will teach us his ways, so that we may walk in his paths." The law will go out from Zion, the word of the LORD from Jerusalem. (Isa. 2:3)

Godly education leads one into the Bible and toward God, not away from him.

The second objection to special, educated leadership flows from our democratic culture, which suggests that many people should lead worship, not just one. This view places a high value on participation and on individual expression that will make the service more interesting and vital. Its adherents often appeal to 1 Corinthians 14:26 as support: "When you come together, everyone has a hymn, or a word of instruction, a revelation, a tongue or an interpretation." Does not such a passage not only justify but actually call for the participation of many in the leadership of worship?

To answer that question we must remember that Paul is writing to a church where things are out of control in worship, and he is reminding them that "God is not a God of disorder but of peace" (1 Cor. 14:33) and that "everything should be done in a fitting and orderly way" (v. 40). More specifically, he is giving advice on how to regulate prophecy and speaking in tongues in worship (see 1 Cor. 14:1-2).

The situation he is describing and regulating reflects the extraordinary days of the early church when the Lord Jesus was still laying the foundations of the church in the work of the apostles and prophets. As Paul wrote to the Ephesians, "You are . . . members of God's household, built on the foundation of the apostles and prophets, with Christ Jesus himself as the chief cornerstone" (Eph. 2:19-20). That foundational work included both the revelation given to the apostles and the special work of the Spirit, such as speaking in tongues, in the church as a whole. Over the years of church history the majority of Christians have believed that just as the office of apostle passed away after that foundation was laid, so the prophecy, miracles, and speaking in tongues that accompanied the apostolic ministry as signs of the apostles' work (2 Cor. 12:12) also passed away.

First Corinthians 14:26, then, is not specific direction for the worship of churches today. Rather, it was direction for those extraordinary first-century times. The abiding responsibility for worship lies with the ongoing office of pastor and teacher that the Lord and his apostles established.

A Spiritual Conversation

The minister leads worship as a conversation between God and the people. In the movement of worship God speaks to his worshipers, and they respond to him. As James reminds us, "Come near to God and he will come near to you" (4:8).

The role of the minister in leading this dialogue between God and his people is sometimes unclear because in worship the minister both speaks for God to the congregation and speaks for the congregation to God. When the minister reads the Bible, preaches, administers the sacraments, or pronounces the benediction, he speaks for God to the congregation. When he offers the pastoral prayer, he speaks for the congregation to God. By the call of God and the congregation, the minister is set aside to these important tasks in worship. It is obvious that in his education, examination, and ordination the minister is set aside to preach. But we should remember that he is also set aside to present the prayers of the congregation to God in words that will please God because they are orthodox and represent the concerns of all.

In his leading role the minister leads the worship of God in a way that keeps the worship faithful and expresses the unity of the people in their meeting with God.

SIX

Music
and Worship

Of all the battles in the worship wars, the battle over music probably has been the most evident and the most emotional. Changes in the style of music have divided, frustrated, and even angered worshipers. Should we sing old hymns or praise choruses? Should the music be classical, traditional, folk, rock, contemporary, country and western, or what? Should we use organs and pianos, or guitars and drums? Is music exclusively for praise in the service, or does it have other functions as well? The amount of time given to music in many services has increased greatly. Some services begin with a lengthy time of singing called "praise and worship," as if singing alone were worship and the rest of the service were something else.

What are we to make of these matters?

A change in music—whether to something older or newer—is difficult because most worshipers are not musicians and simply like what is familiar to them. Most worshipers are not motivated by some aesthetic theory, but by the emotional links they have to their familiar music. Because music so powerfully engages and expresses our emotions, it is not surprising that it is an emotional minefield for individuals and congregations.

As with all ways of worship, we must evaluate music in the first place biblically. We must stand back from our own experiences and preferences and ask again, "What pleases God?" We should recognize that not all music and praise pleases him. Think of the worship and praise that Israel offered to God in the wilderness at Mount Sinai. They made a golden calf, called it the Lord, and danced around it (Exod. 32:4-6). Such praise was an abomination to God and evoked his wrath! We must carefully seek what the Bible says about how we should praise the Lord and make music to him.

When we think of music in the worship of God, we are really thinking of three issues: 1) the words that we sing, 2) the tunes to which we sing those words, and 3) the instruments we might use to accompany the singing.

The Words We Sing

Of these three issues the first is the most important. The words we take upon our lips to sing to God must be true and pleasing to him. The Cambridge Declaration reminds us that one of the problems we face today is what we sing: "Pastors have neglected their rightful oversight of worship, including the doctrinal content of music." How can we be sure that the words we sing please God? God has given us direction by giving us in the Bible a whole book as a model for what we are to sing. The Book of Psalms (which in Hebrew is entitled the Book of Praises) provides us with songs that God himself has inspired. The Psalms should at least function as the model for what we as Christians sing to God.

The Songs We Use

What do the Psalms teach about song? First, they remind us of the rich variety of songs that we can and should present to God. The Psalms contain joyful praise and thanksgiving. The Psalms are called the Book of Praises because they not only contain but also culminate in the praise of God (see especially Pss. 146—150.) But the Psalms contain more than praise. Some Psalms reflect on creation (for example, Pss. 19 and 104); others recount the great saving work of God in Christ (Pss. 2, 22, 24, and 110); still others meditate on the perfections of God's revealed Word (especially Ps. 119). There are Psalms of lamentation and repentance (Pss. 32, 51, and 137) as well as Psalms that express the confusion and frustration that God's people sometimes experience living in this fallen world (Pss. 44 and 73). John Calvin rightly observed about the Psalter, "There is not an emotion of which any one can be conscious that is not here presented as in a mirror."

In some churches today it seems that only happy, joyful songs are sung. But joy is not the only emotion that Christians experience. Christian worship needs to provide times when sad or reflective emotions are expressed as well as happy ones. A variety of song texts, as we find them in the Psalter, are crucial for that purpose.

Second, the Psalms also model for us the substance of our singing. A few Psalms are short and have repetitive elements, but most are full, rich, profound responses to God and his work. Singing praise to God, the Psalter reminds us, is not just emotional expression, but a real engagement of the mind. Songs that are very repetitive or shallow and sentimental do not follow the model of the Psalter. The command to love God with all our mind must inform our singing. Mind and emotions together are the model of praise presented to us in the Psalms, and the modern church must work at restoring that union where it has been lost.

Once we recapture a proper sense of the texts we ought to sing, the other two issues about singing are relatively easy to resolve. What tunes shall we sing? We may use any tune that is singable for a congregation and that supports the content of the song. The tune should reflect the mood and substance of the song in light of the joy and reverence that are appropriate to worship. With those guidelines in mind (and a sensitivity to the congregation's difficulty with change), the issue of tunes for songs should be resolved smoothly.

What Kind of Instruments?

What kind of musical accompaniment is biblical? In Old Testament worship a wide range of instruments was used in the worship of the temple. Yet in the worship of the church it appears that for almost the first thousand years of its history no instruments were used in Christian worship. Today most churches use one or more instruments. But where instruments are used, the instruments should aid the singing of the congregation, not overwhelm it. They should contribute to a deep spirit of reverence and joy, not undermine it.

Nowhere in the New Testament church are instruments clearly used for worship. They certainly have no central or independent role in worship. At most they should support the singing that the congregation is commanded to do. If that is their purpose, rock bands would be clearly inappropriate for Christian worship, but either an organ or a guitar might be used.

Music is a powerful and vital element in the worship life of God's people. But precisely because it is so significant, we need to give careful thought to it. We must be sure that we are pleasing God and not entertaining ourselves. The temptation to turn worship into entertainment is great because as sinners we are much more inclined to be self-centered than God-centered. We are much more inclined to amuse ourselves than to serve God.

SEVEN

Entertainment, Evangelism, and Worship

The call for entertainment in worship in our time is often cast in a particularly seductive form. Entertainment is often sold in the name of evangelism. We are told that we must make worship interesting and exciting for the unconverted so that they will come to church and be converted. At first glance that argument is very appealing. We all want to see many brought to faith in Christ. Who wants to be against evangelism? But we must remember: entertainment is not evangelism, and evangelism is not worship. People are evangelized, not by a juggler, but by the presentation of the Gospel. And while evangelism may occur in worship as the Gospel is faithfully proclaimed, the purpose and focus of worship is that those who believe in Christ should gather and meet with God.

In 1 Corinthians 14:24-25 the apostle Paul comments on the presence of an unbeliever in a worship service. He does not call for the church to entertain the unbeliever or make him feel comfortable. Rather, in the clear and understandable articulation of the truth, the unbeliever should be convinced that he is a sinner. "So he will fall down and worship God, exclaiming, 'God is really among you!'" Faithful worship, where the primary purpose is the meeting of God with his people through his Word, may well have the secondary result that unbelievers will come to faith. But worship must not be constructed for the unbeliever. Rather, it is for God and the church.

The whole service in the church, then, must not be shaped for either entertainment or evangelism. Instead, it must serve to unite the people of God for their meeting with God.

EIGHT

Worshiping with the Heart

We have focused much of our attention in this book on the forms or externals of corporate worship. But we must remember that such forms are at the most only half of the story. The most faithful, biblical forms will not guarantee true worship. Using good forms may only mean that we are formalists, going through the motions in worship. Jesus quoted Isaiah as saying, "These people honor me with their lips, but their hearts are far from me" (Matt. 15:8). In a similar vein Paul warned against those "having a form of godliness but denying its power" (2 Tim. 3:5). True worship occurs when we worship with the heart.

Preparing for Worship

To meet with God we need to come to worship prepared. We need to come well-rested, expectant, thoughtfully ready to meet with God. We need to be aware that God will be present in the elements of worship that he has appointed. He will be present to speak through his Word and will be present to hear our praise and prayers. We need to come with clear understanding of the ways in which worship with God's people will bless us and should come looking for that blessing.

We come to worship in faith. Faith is trusting Christ, resting in his finished work for the forgiveness of our sins. Our faith must be real as we come to church, so that our reliance on Christ may deepen. We come to worship with repentance, acknowledging that we are sinners and seeking the grace of God so that we more and more turn from sin and pursue holiness. We come to worship with love for God and for his people. Such love will make us desire communion with the people of God and long to draw nearer to God.

> I rejoiced with those who
>   said to me,
> "Let us go to the house of
>   the LORD." (Ps. 122:1)

When the heart is prepared for and engaged in worship, we can enter into the sentiments of the Psalmist:

> Teach me your way, O LORD,
> and I will walk in your truth;
> give me an undivided heart,
> that I may fear your name.
> I will praise you, O LORD my God,
> with all my heart;
> I will glorify your name forever.
> For great is your love toward me;
> you have delivered my soul from the
> depths of the grave. (Ps. 86:11-13)

> Search me, O God, and know my heart:
> test me and know my anxious thoughts.
> See if there is any offensive way in me,
> and lead me in the way
>   everlasting. (Ps. 139:23-24)

> I will praise you, O LORD, with all my heart;
> before the "gods" I will sing your praise.
> I will bow down toward your holy temple
> and will praise your name

for your love and your faithfulness,
for you have exalted above all things
your name and your word. (Ps. 138:1-2)

When the heart is prepared by the Word of God and by God's Spirit for worship, then the worship we desire is the worship that delights God. We come not to be pleased, but to offer God the worship that pleases him. We move from the self-centeredness that characterizes those who do not know God, to the God-centeredness that should characterize those who do know him.

Evaluating Worship

With so many approaches to worship and so much variety from church to church, the Christian must become an evaluator of worship. The question "How should we worship?" is inevitably linked to the question "Where should we worship?" Once we know what pleases God in worship, we need to be where such worship occurs.

To evaluate worship properly, you need to begin with yourself. You need self-evaluation. You need to ask the following of yourself:

• How much do I know about what the Bible says about worship?

• Who can help me learn more about biblical worship?

• Do I want above all to draw near to God in worship?

• Do I want to please God rather than myself in worship?

• Do I understand my responsibility to worship God with his people regularly?

• Will I seek God's will in worship while avoiding a judgmental and legalistic spirit toward others?

You also need to ask these questions about the worship of any church you plan to attend:

• Does this church love and believe the Bible?

• Is the worship of this church filled with the Word of God?

• How much of the service is given to the reading of the Bible?

• How much of the service is given to biblical prayer?

• How much of the service is given to singing that is biblical in content and character?

• What is the content of the preaching?

• Is preaching a substantial part of the service?

• Is the Law of God clearly present in the service?

• Is the Gospel of Jesus Christ clearly expressed and central in the service?

• What is the role of the sacraments in the ministry of the church?

• Are there elements of the service that are more entertaining than biblical?

• Are both joyful thanksgiving and reverent awe expressed and balanced in the service?

We cannot be casual about matters of worship. They are too important. We need to be thoughtful and biblical. To do that we need to shoulder our personal responsibility to study and pray about worship. We should seek help from faithful ministers and friends. And we must seek a church where worship is faithful to God's Word.

An Invitation to Worship

In this study we have thought together about worship in a variety of ways. But at the end we must remember that God wants us to worship him.

Come, let us bow down in worship,
let us kneel before the LORD our Maker;
for he is our God
and we are the people of his pasture,
the flock under his care. (Ps. 95:6-7)

We need to heed that call to worship and to iden-
tify with a congregation that worships faithfully. We
must worship in a way that pleases God, for our
God is a consuming fire.

FOR FURTHER
READING

Burroughs, Jeremiah. *Gospel Worship*. Ligonier, Pa.: Soli Deo Gloria, 1990. Original edition 1648.

Bushell, Michael. *The Songs of Zion*. Pittsburgh: Crown and Covenant, 1993. Second edition.

Davies, Horton. *The Worship of the English Puritans*. Ligonier, Pa.: Soli Deo Gloria, 1997.

Dawn, Marva. *Reaching Out Without Dumbing Down*. Grand Rapids, Mich.: Eerdmans, 1995.

Henry, Matthew. *A Method for Prayer,* ed. J. Ligon Duncan, III. Greenville, S.C.: Reformed Academic Press, 1994.

Johnson, Terry, ed. *Leading in Worship*. Oak Ridge, Tenn.: Covenant Foundation, 1996.

Old, Hughes Oliphant. *Worship*. Atlanta: John Knox Press, 1984.

Rayburn, Robert. *O Come, Let Us Worship*. Grand Rapids, Mich.: Baker, 1980.